Nasty Things, Murders

A play for women

ARTHUR LOVEGROVE

SAMUEL FRENCH

LONDON
NEW YORK TORONTO SYDNEY HOLLYWOOD

CHARACTERS

Ethel
Louise
Madge
Mary
The Matron

The action takes place on a winter's evening in the lounge of the Grantley Home for Retired Gentlewomen

Time – the present

NASTY THINGS, MURDERS

The lounge of the Grantley Home for Retired Gentlewomen. A winter's evening

It is a comfortably furnished room with a large settee in front of which is a television set, with the back facing the audience, standing on a small table. There are two armchairs, one slightly apart. In the back wall are windows across which curtains are drawn, and against another wall is an escritoire on top of which is a telephone. A door leads off to the hall

The CURTAIN *rises to reveal four old ladies, all in their late sixties or early seventies. They are all dressed in a manner which can be described as neat but not gaudy—not too smart but certainly far from shabby. They wear their favourite pieces of jewellery and each has a handbag or reticule. In fact, they look what they are— retired gentlefolk. Ethel, sardonic and rather aristocratic; Madge, a short, tubby woman; Louise, smallish and excitable; and Mary, gentle and sweet looking*

Ethel is standing in front of the television set banging it with her hand. Madge and Louise are seated side by side on the settee facing it, and Mary is seated in the armchair which is slightly away from the others, placidly knitting

Ethel (*with a final vicious bang on top of the set*) There! (*She steps back and surveys it*)

Louise Not a thing! Oh, this is infuriating! (*She bangs her clenched hands on her knees in exasperation*) Oh, why did it have to go wrong then!

Madge Try the left-hand side slightly above the middle, dear.

Ethel I've banged everywhere. How could I have missed the left-hand side slightly above the middle! If I have, it's the only part I haven't thumped apart from the screen, and I'd like to put my foot through that.

Madge From past experience I've found that if you bang it there you jar the thingummybob attached to the whatsit.

Ethel Do you have to be so technical, Madge?

Louise Oh, can't somebody *do* something, please! We must know how it ends. (*Again she bangs her fists on her knees in annoyance*)

Madge Let me try, Ethel dear. (*She rises*)

Ethel You're the expert, be my guest. (*She steps back and reseats herself on the settee*)

Madge goes to the set and carefully selects her spot with the precision of a surgeon about to make an incision. She suddenly hits it sharply twice and steps back to survey the result

Louise There! Nothing! Ooooooh, I could scream!

Madge That's odd, it's always worked before.

Ethel Perhaps your diagnosis was wrong. It's probably the howdoyoudo attached to the whatdoyoucallit that's gone, and God only knows where they are.

Madge We'll have to get Matron to ring the service department.

Louise And what good will that do?

Ethel They'll send a mechanic along and Madge will baffle him with technicalities.

Louise (*wailing*) But that won't be until tomorrow and we will have missed the programme.

Madge Never mind, Louise, they'll probably repeat it. They always do.

Louise But I can't possibly wait that long. Oooooh, I could scream! I won't be able to sleep tonight wondering who did it.

Madge (*comfortably*) Never mind, dear, I'll give you one of my sleeping tablets.

Louise But I do mind. I love mysteries.

Ethel Then you should be in your element because you are now mystified.

Louise But I must know who did it. Oooooh, that—that—beastly set would go wrong tonight. Can't anybody remember the case?

Madge I never remember murders, not even big ones, and this one happened twenty years ago.

Ethel I can't even remember a murder that happened last month. If it comes to that I can't always remember what I did last week.

Madge In any case, why should we remember? Even the BBC didn't expect us to,

Ethel That's why they call the series *Little Known Murderers*, and if the BBC considers them little known, they must be. And don't forget, although the facts and circumstances were the same, they pointed out that the names had been changed.

Madge Why?

Ethel To spare the feelings of surviving relatives, I suppose.

Louise What does it matter about the names! It was the murder and it was so interesting. They do that series so awfully well with actors re-enacting the roles. It really was just like a detective story with all the suspects. Ooooh, I could scream with vexation!

Ethel That's the third time you've said that. Why don't you let one go then you could relax, in fact, we all could!

Louise Well, I'm annoyed! (*She bangs a cushion viciously*) It's like having the last pages of a book torn out. I tell you I won't be able to sleep tonight.

Madge Never mind, dear, I'll let you have two of my sleeping pills. Now where are the playing cards?

Ethel (*picking up the newspaper beside her*) In the desk.

Madge goes across to the escritoire, opens a drawer and takes out a pack of cards. She then goes and seats herself in the other arm-chair and proceeds to lay out the cards for patience on a little table in front of her

Louise (*suddenly*) Now why should anyone want to murder that nice old lady?

Ethel (*idly turning the newspaper pages*) Money, I suppose. They said she was rolling in it.

Louise But who was most likely to profit by her death?

Ethel Apart from the undertaker I really wouldn't know.

Madge (*busy with her cards*) They did say quite a few people had high hopes of a substantial legacy.

Louise That's right! Now there was her doctor who had been attending her for years.

Madge They didn't say who was going to benefit specifically.

Louise Don't be silly, dear, old widows like that, typical hypochondriacs, always leave money to their doctors.

Ethel I wouldn't leave any to mine, and I'd tell him so. Too much of an inducement for an overdose.

Louise Then there was her nephew.

Ethel Always a chief suspect, and my bet for this murder. I wouldn't trust mine an inch.

Louise But there were quite a few relatives.

Ethel Like vultures hovering. Thank God I've outlived mine.

Madge Except your nephew.

Ethel At the rate he's going with fast women and fast cars I'll outlive him too.

Louise Then there was the paid companion.

Ethel Paid companions must be subconscious masochists. Always at an old girl's beck and call day and night. Y'know, I'm sure I'd lead mine, if I had one, a dog's life just like she did.

Louise (*shocked*) Oh, no, not that dear old lady. Mrs—Mrs— what *was* her name?

Mary Lester, Mrs Caroline Lester. At least, that's the name she was given in the play.

They all turn and look at Mary in surprise. They had obviously forgotten she was there

Louise Of course, Mary, Mrs Caroline Lester. Such a sweet old lady.

Mary (*placidly knitting*) She wasn't, you know.

Louise Wasn't?

Mary Oh, no! That was the impression she gave.

Madge Impression she gave?

Mary Oh, yes! That was what came over in the play. Quite wrong!

Ethel Was it?

Mary Oh, yes, quite wrong. Beverly Nicholls wrote a book once called *Are They The Same At Home?* Such an apt title I always thought. (*She holds up her knitting and surveys it*) People aren't you know. They put on an outdoor façade as soon as they go through their front door. In the same way they put on an indoor façade as soon as visitors arrive.

Ethel Yes, I suppose, when you come to think of it, we all do really in some form or another.

Mary So you really never get to *know* a person until you live with them.

Louise But we're all living together here.

Mary Yes, interesting, isn't it! (*There is a pause as she consults*

her knitting pattern pamphlet) Ah, now I must decrease one
stitch at each end of the next row and every sixth row.
Ethel (*slightly stupefied*) You do that!
Louise (*excitedly*) Then you obviously knew Mrs Lester.

For a moment Mary's busy fingers are still, then she speaks quietly

Mary Oh, yes, Louise, I knew her.
Louise But this is wonderful! Did you know her well?
Mary Very well, unfortunately. She was a mean, spiteful, bitter
old woman, believe me.
Louise Oh, no!
Madge This is a surprise. How could you have sat there so quiet
without saying a word?
Mary It's very easy to keep quiet over something you'd rather
forget.
Ethel Then why speak now?

*Mary drops her knitting on her lap as if puzzled. After a moment
she replies*

Mary I don't know! Oh, yes, I suppose I do. It was Louise's
conviction that she was such a sweet old lady that made me
forget myself. They say that one should never speak ill of the
dead, but to be truthful, one's opinion of a person while living
should not be changed by their passing. They cannot claim
virtues by death that they never possessed in life.
Ethel That's very true.
Mary Oh, dear, I've talked too much. Let's drop the subject.
Louise Oh, no! You can't stop now. That's worse than the television set breaking down.
Ethel Knowing Louise she'll pester you until she gets the truth.
Louise (*indignantly*) Now, Ethel, that's not fair! Mary hasn't
been here long and you are giving her the wrong impression
about me. I'm not like that at all.
Mary I'm sure you're not.
Louise There! And just to prove it I won't say another word on
the subject.

*Louise, obviously controlling herself and longing to continue the
discussion, sits gazing ahead. Madge stops playing patience and
looks covertly at Mary. Ethel turns the pages of her paper without
looking at them. There is a long pause while Mary placidly knits*

Madge (*suddenly breaking the silence*) Mary!

Ethel flings her paper aside and she and Louise both turn to Madge

Mary Yes?

Madge I really am quite a nice person . . .

Mary I know you are.

Madge (*suddenly chuckling*) Curiosity killed the cat. I've never really known what it was curious about, but three old ladies are going to suffer the same fate.

Louise (*eagerly*) And we really are sorry.

Ethel I fail to see that it is any business of ours——

Louise Ethel!

Ethel —but it's no good, Mary. I'm just a nosey, interfering old woman like the others. But don't blame us, blame yourself.

Madge No, blame the television. If it hadn't broken down we would have watched the programme and then promptly forgotten it.

Louise But as it is . . .

Mary Oh, dear, you're quite right. It is my fault, I shouldn't have spoken. But it is sometimes hard to keep things to yourself. It's harder still to forget.

Madge And sometimes easier to talk.

Mary And then regret having spoken. (*She lays her knitting down on her lap*) Was it really twenty years ago? I remember it as though it was yesterday. She, Caroline, lived in a lovely old house called "The Beeches", which I always thought peculiar as the only trees around were oaks. It was quite a full house. Caroline, her personal maid, her paid companion, her nurse, her staff consisting of a cook and housemaid, and her sister. Oh, and her nephew, her late brother's son, was staying for the weekend.

Louise Yes, they were all in the play, including the doctor who called.

Mary And like the fictitious names they were given they were equally unlike their real life prototypes. Caroline, as I said, was a mean, selfish, spiteful old woman. Her maid at the time, she never kept one for long, was a gay, flighty thing. Being bed-ridden Caroline had a nurse, a very clinical, no nonsense person. I suppose it was because she was so very clinical that Caroline never got under her skin. Her unmarried sister lived with her, and like everyone else was dependent on Caroline who had married well. Her late husband had left her quite a fortune. Her nephew paid his duty visits, one couldn't blame him as he had expectations, and they were worth the inconvenience and his aunt's bad temper. The murder took place . . .

Louise But what about the paid companion?

A slight pause

Mary Ah, yes, the paid companion. Just as you said, Ethel, Caroline led her a dog's life. The proverbial "whipping boy", so to speak. "Mary do this, Mary do that! Where are my spectacles? Find them!"

Madge Mary? In the play she was called Maud.

A quick glance between Ethel, Madge and Louise

Mary Oh, yes, so she was. So confusing with the fictitious names and the real ones. Maud, yes! Where was I?

Ethel The paid companion led a dog's life . . .

Louise And you said the murder took place . . .

Mary On the Sunday night, or rather in the early hours of the Monday morning. That week-end was terribly hot, so very hot and still. So hot that one's nerves were on edge waiting for the storm, which was bound to come, to break and bring relief. Caroline was at her worst. Nothing that anyone did was right, so everybody gave her a wide berth. Except the paid companion. When you're in that position you just have to put up with it—that's what you're paid for. Just before midnight the nurse went to see Caroline to make sure that all was well. The companion was there. She had been summoned to read to her mistress. Carline's taste in literature wasn't exactly of the highest order. It was extraordinary that such a woman should enjoy what can only be described as sugary romances. Ethel M. Dell was her favourite author and it was one of her books that Mary—er—Maud was reading to her that night. The night was hot, airless, and heavy. Mary had a blinding headache, but she couldn't tell Caroline that. Having been dismissed, the nurse left them. Shortly after that the storm broke. Such a storm, it raged all night as though the very heavens were at war.

*Mary pauses and gazes in front of her as though lost in her thoughts.
The others sit quite still as though not daring to breathe. Suddenly
Mary recollects herself and continues as though she had never
stopped*

The nurse went back to her patient the next morning at seven
o'clock and found her dead.

Louise How?

Mary Caroline had a heart complaint and at first it was thought
she had suffered an attack. But the doctor was suspicious and
there was a post-mortem. She had been smothered.

Ethel Smothered?

Mary (*nodding her head*) With one of her pillows.

Louise But who did it?

Ethel The nephew!

Mary (*after a pause*) No, the paid companion.

Madge Mary—I mean Maud?

Mary begins placidly to knit again

Ethel But how did—how did . . . ?

Mary How did they find out?

Ethel Yes, that it was the companion. Did she confess?

Mary Oh, no! The police are very clever and she was incredibly
stupid. A person being smothered naturally struggles and tries
to claw the arms holding the pillow away. The companion was
foolishly wearing her red woollen cardigan at the time and
the police found traces of the red wool under Caroline's
finger-nails.

Madge (*carefully*) Then Mary, I mean Maud, must have been a
very big strong woman.

Mary No, quite the opposite. Quite small and gentle. But fury
lends strength and Caroline was rather old.

There is another pause

Louise What happened to her?

Mary She, of course, protested her innocence. Swore that when
she left Caroline she was alive. But the evidence was too strong
and she was found guilty, but the jury put in a strong plea for
mercy.

Louise And?

Mary She went to prison. She served her sentence and was
released a few years ago.

Again a pause as the others look at each other

Ethel Why did she do it? I mean, did she have expectations of a
legacy?

Mary (*carefully laying down her knitting and rolling it up to put
it in her reticule*) She may have done. But I really think that
everything got too much for her. A sudden rage caused by
constant nagging from a mean, selfish old woman. She paid
for it bitterly, paid in years for a moment's blind rage. It's
funny how the gentlest of people can suddenly find they cannot
take any more and something snaps. (*Having put her knitting
away she looks at her watch*) Goodness me! Nearly nine o'clock.
I must go to my room. There's an orchestral concert on the
radio and I do so enjoy good music. (*She rises and goes to the
door*)

Louise I suppose the nephew, the whole family in fact, profited
by her death.

Mary (*turning at the door*) Oh, no, none of them got a penny,
not a single, solitary penny. She left it all to the Church. I
think she thought by doing that it was a useful insurance for
the hereafter. She really was a mean, spiteful old woman. So
Louise, the paid companion did it—so you won't need Madge's
sleeping pills after all.

Mary exits and closes the door

The others gaze at the door for a moment, then look at one another

Louise (*expressively*) Well!!

Madge (*gathering up her cards*) I've gone off patience. (*She rises,
goes to the escritoire and puts the pack away*)

Louise (*in horror*) But who'd have thought it!

Ethel (*calmly*) Thought what?

Louise (*utterly amazed*) Thought what? Are you mad?

Ethel No, and I'm not gullible either.

Louise Don't you realize we have a murderess in our midst?

Madge I don't really think . . .

Ethel Nonsense!

Louise How can you say it's nonsense! She *told* us, didn't she!

Ethel Louise, don't be so quick in jumping to conclusions. She told us the end of a story that the television didn't.

Madge (*relieved*) That's right! Of course, she remembered the case.

Louise What? Twenty years ago?

Ethel Why not? It's quite possible.

Louise But how did she know all the details and the people? That bit about the storm and Mary's nagging headache. (*Triumphantly*) There! Mary! Mary! *Her* name. She slipped up there.

Ethel (*exasperated*) The names were fictitious. Mary, Maud, May! Easy enough to make a mistake. You listened to the programme. What was the name of that sister of Caroline's that lived with her? Come on, tell me that!

Louise It was—was—Emily.

Madge Are you sure? I thought it was Lucy.

Ethel There, you've both forgotten. Lucy was the maid. The sister was called Amy. I only remember that because it was my mother's name. Easy enough to mistake Maud for Mary.

Louise (*obstinately*) You can't convince me. It wasn't a mistake. She knew and slipped up over her own name. She said Mary was a small woman——

Madge (*doubtfully*) —and gentle.

Louise And Mary's gentle. At least, I thought so. I don't care what you say, she knew too much.

Ethel You are being utterly ridiculous. You don't find murderesses in a respectable place like this.

Louise Where do you find them? They have to live somewhere.

Ethel But not here.

Louise Why not?

Ethel Because Mary was playing a joke on us.

Louise A joke?

Ethel Yes! I'm sure she is up in her room now laughing to herself knowing what we're thinking. At least, what you're thinking, Louise. She did it deliberately for your benefit.

Louise (*outraged*) Mine!

Ethel Yes! Keeping on and on about how you wanted to scream because you didn't know the ending. If you had gone on much longer for two pins I would have given you an ending. I would have told you the nephew did it, as I'm convinced he did. A most unpleasant type.

Louise She also said the actors were quite unlike their real-life prototypes.

Ethel In that case the companion was probably a thoroughly hefty wench.

Madge What's the time?

Ethel (*glancing at her watch*) Just gone nine. Why?

Madge Well, that programme finished at nine.

Ethel Well?

Madge I was thinking. Perhaps we could ring up the BBC and say our set broke down and could they tell us who did it.

Ethel And we'll find it was the nephew.

Louise (*rising and scurrying across to the telephone*) Of course! Oh, Madge, you are clever, what a good idea. (*She picks up a directory and starts looking through it*) They will tell us then we'll really know. Ah, here it is! (*She lifts the receiver and dials the number*) It's ringing.

Ethel It was the nephew.

Madge I didn't like the nurse. So hard and unsympathetic.

Louise I'm sure . . . (*On the phone*) Oh, hallo! BBC? . . . I'm sorry to trouble you but our television set broke down . . . What? . . . I know you don't do repairs. We, my friends and I, were watching that programme *Little Known Murderers* when it happened . . . Yes, most infuriating. Well, we just wanted to know who did it . . . Who? . . . Johnson Jarvis?

Madge There was nobody named Jarvis . . .

Louise (*on the phone*) Who was he? . . . Oh, the producer! No, not him! Who did the murder? . . . Oh, thank you. (*To the others*) They're going to find out.

Madge Going to find out? You'd think they'd watch their own programmes.

Ethel I doubt whether the girl on the switchboard has the time.

Louise (*on the phone*) Yes, I'm still here . . . Oh, how very kind of you . . . Mr Jarvis? I'm so sorry to trouble you but our TV set broke down . . . Yes, most unfortunate. We very much wanted to know who did the murder in your programme *Little Known Murderers* tonight . . . Who? (*With a little shriek*) Oh, my God! (*She slams down the receiver and turns and looks at the others in horror*) It was the companion!

Madge Oh, no!

Ethel (*shaken*) Even that doesn't prove that . . .

Louise How much more proof do you want? I shan't sleep to-night. Tonight? I shan't sleep soundly here again.

Ethel You've slept soundly the three months Mary's been with us.

Louise Will you?

Ethel Of course.

Louise I shall lock my door.

Ethel (*exasperated*) You always do.

Louise I'll put a chair against it now.

Madge But she won't do it again. She was provoked before.

Ethel So don't nag her.

Louise (*triumphantly*) There! What did Madge say! She won't do it again, she was provoked before. Now you believe it, Madge.

Madge (*distraught*) Perhaps! Oh, I don't know! I'm not sure.

Ethel This is becoming utterly ridiculous . . .

Louise (*raising her voice*) Ridiculous? It had the ring of truth to me and the BBC have told us it was true. How did she know the actors weren't like the real people? Tell me that? How did she *know*?

Ethel Louise! Will you be quiet!

Louise Quiet? How can you stand there . . .

Madge The trouble is we can't be *absolutely* sure . . .

Louise Sure? She *told* us! (*Spacing out and emphasizing each word*) She—sat—there—and—told—us! Oh, my God, this has brought on my palpitations!

Ethel Well, for heaven's sake sit down and shut up!

Madge What do we know about her?

Louise (*sitting down and patting her bosom*) Enough, more than enough now. Oh, these palpitations!

Ethel If we hadn't watched that programme or the set hadn't broken down we would never have known.

Louise There! You said we would never have known. Even you have doubts now.

Ethel I haven't! I mean, I have! Oh, heavens, you're getting me confused now.

Madge She's been here three months.

Louise Exactly! We know nothing about her. Where did she come from? What was she?

Madge You know, I must admit she does keep herself to herself.

Ethel In heaven's name, is that a crime? She's a nice, sweet, gentle old lady.

Louise They all said Crippen was.

Ethel They've said many things about Crippen but never once that he was a nice, sweet, gentle old lady.

Louise You know what I mean.

Ethel Yes, and I know what trouble you're going to cause.

Louise Me? Cause trouble?

Ethel Yes. We have got to keep this to ourselves.

Louise (*dumfounded*) Keep this to our . . . (*Exploding*) What about everybody else here?

Ethel All we've been told is a story of something that happened twenty years ago.

Louise With what one could only describe as artistic embellishments. All right! All right! *If* it's a story then there can be no harm in repeating it so that everyone can enjoy it.

Ethel I can imagine you at breakfast bringing it up in conversation. Before we've cracked our boiled eggs you'll have the rest of the residents thinking they're dining with the Borgia's.

Louise You don't dine at breakfast and the Borgia's used poison, they didn't smother with pillows.

Ethel What I am trying to impress upon you is that we have no proof. *Proof!*

Louise (*to Madge*) No proof she says.

Ethel She never said it *was* her.

Louise And she never said it *wasn't.*

Ethel I want proof positive.

Louise Like one of us being found smothered in bed one morning?

The Matron enters. She is a big, stout, motherly woman of about fifty-five

Matron (*breezily*) Hallo! I expected you to be watching television.

Ethel (*hastily*) We were, but it broke down.

Matron Broke down? What happened?

Ethel Madge is of the opinion that it is the thingummybob attached to the whatsit.

Matron (*laughing*) I wouldn't be at all surprised. I'll ring the rental company in the morning and get them to send a repair man along. You must have spent a dull evening.

Louise I wouldn't say that. In fact, it's been far from dull.

Ethel We've been chatting.

Matron That does make a change from watching the box. I always say television has killed the art of conversation, but you've all had a nice change. As Louise just said, it was far from dull. (*She moves to the chair where Mary had sat and straightens the cushion*) What were you chatting about?

Ethel (*quickly*) Oh—er—life in general.

Louise And death.

Matron You must have had a riotous evening. Couldn't you have thought of a more cheerful subject?

Louise Well, we were watching that programme *Little Known Murderers* when the set broke down.

Madge And in the story an old lady was murdered . . .

Louise By another old lady.

Matron Really? Well, thank heaven nothing like that will happen here. (*Laughing*) Old ladies murdering each other. I've never heard such nonsense.

Ethel Unfortunately true. It was a real murder that happened twenty years ago.

Matron Did it? Nasty things, murders. You really would think they could put on more cheerful programmes. People want entertainment in the evenings. A jolly good laugh. Not old ladies killing each other.

Louise Actually it was very interesting.

Matron Ah well, it gave you something to talk about even if it was morbid. I'll get that set repaired first thing in the morning. (*She goes to the door*)

Louise Matron!

Matron (*stopping and turning*) Yes, Louise?

Louise (*casually*) Mary was with us.

Matron I'm glad. She hasn't been here long and it's good for her to get to know you all.

Madge She's a very quiet person, isn't she?

Matron Yes, but very sweet.

Madge Oh, yes.

Louise She never says much. I mean . . .

Ethel She keeps herself to herself.

Matron A little shy I expect. Some people are like that.
Louise What was she? I mean, before she came here.
Matron She was what is known as a lady's companion.

The others react

Louise Oh!
Matron I think that's so very sad on both sides. That one should be rich enough and yet so lonely that one has to pay for a companion, and that one should be so poor and lonely to have to accept such a position. Don't you agree?
Ethel Very true.
Louise Where did she come from?
Matron I really don't know. She did say she spent some years abroad.
Louise (*rising abruptly from the settee*) Abroad?

The others react

Madge (*involuntary*) Oh, dear, that must have been when . . . (*She suddenly stops*)
Matron (*curiously*) Must have been when?
Louise Did she say how long she'd been abroad?
Matron About ten years. She came back a few years ago. Why?
Louise (*collapsing on the settee*) Oh, my God, it *is* true!
Matron If she told you she'd been abroad it is true.
Louise That's it—it isn't! (*Thumping her chest*) Now my palpitations have started again. I shan't sleep tonight.
Ethel (*warningly*) Louise!
Louise (*snapping*) Don't "Louise" me. We'll all be murdered in our beds.
Matron (*shocked amazement*) Mercy me! Murdered? (*She collapses in the armchair*)
Ethel It's some stupid idea that Louise has got into her head.
Louise It is not stupid, she told us.
Matron Told you what? For heaven's sake tell me!
Ethel It was that documentary play tonight about a murder of an old lady twenty years ago . . .
Louise And the paid companion did it.
Matron But what's that got to do with Mary?
Louise She did it! She said so!

Ethel She didn't! She never said, "I did the murder!" Did she? Did she?

Louise She didn't have to. She knew all the details, even the minutest ones, and she knew everybody.

Matron Well, she might have done. Known the people, I mean.

Louise Not the way she described it. It was positively eerie. Made my blood run cold.

Matron But she might have known the people, or even been very slightly connected with them, therefore she is bound to know more about it than was reported in the press, for example. And she came here with the strongest recommendations.

Louise Forged!

Ethel Don't be stupid, Louise, Matron is quite right.

Louise Not in this case. Oh, no! I could tell by the look in her eyes.

Ethel You're so short-sighted I doubt whether you could see her eyes.

Matron But if she's been abroad . . .

Louise Of course she wasn't abroad. She'd been in prison.

Matron In prison?

Louise Of course, serving her sentence. She couldn't tell anyone that so she said she'd been abroad. Matron, you'll have to do something.

Matron Do something? Do what?

Louise (*amazed*) Do what?

Ethel Yes, Louise, do what?

Louise Are you all mad?

Ethel I'm not, and I'm pretty certain Matron and Madge aren't, so that leaves you.

Louise You won't say I'm mad when you wake up in bed one morning and find yourself murdered.

Ethel If I've been murdered I can't wake up!

Louise Don't be so pedantic. You know what I mean.

Madge I think Louise means . . .

Louise (*icily*) Thank you, Madge, I don't need you to tell me or the others what I mean. I am quite capable of speaking for myself.

Ethel After the last half an hour nobody will deny that!

Louise rises and moves across to the Matron. She is controlling herself with difficulty, and therefore speaks with great deliberation

Louise Matron, twenty years ago a woman who was a paid companion murdered her mistress cold-bloodedly. A resident here knew all the details, some so intimate that only the murderer could possibly know them. She even described the physical appearance of the murderess, but worst of all—she slipped up over the name. She called her Mary, *her* name, and she was a paid companion. You should have been here when she told her story. She served a term of imprisonment for her crime and comes here with a cock-and-bull story about having been abroad. All right, I'll concede that what happened once won't happen again. But, and here is the crux of the matter, we can't possibly keep this to ourselves however much we try, it's bound to come out sometime. We are bound to regard her with deep suspicion. Can you imagine the effect of this revelation on the other residents? If old Mrs Barnes had been here tonight she'd have died on the spot! As Matron of this home the welfare of *all* the residents is your responsibility. The decision is yours. (*She turns and reseats herself determinedly on the settee*) I have nothing more to say.

Ethel I wish I could believe that.

Louise You cannot provoke me, Ethel, I have stated my case.

Madge I hate to say this, but I think Louise is right.

Matron (*rising and moving distractedly about the room*) This is terrible, I don't know what to say. Even if what you tell me is true, I mean, I'm sure all this happened as you described it. . . . Well, I can't go up to Mary and say, "Are you a murderess?"

Louise Of course you can't. She'd deny it. Say it was a joke.

Ethel As it very well might be.

Matron Ethel, can you honestly imagine Mary joking about a subject like that? It's a type of—of—sick humour that I'm sure she isn't capable of. It's not like her. Even you'll admit that, won't you?

Ethel is silent

You see, you can't answer. Oh, dear, she's such a pleasant little body. (*Appealingly*) Look, my dears, can you be sure?

Absolutely sure! This is far too serious to have a single doubt.

Louise Yes, I'm sure—absolutely.

Matron Madge?

Madge Oh, dear, I hate to say this, but she was so convincing. Yes!

Matron Ethel?

Ethel But why *tell* us?

Madge She did say that it's sometimes hard to keep things to yourself——

Louise —and it's harder still to forget. Now even you can't deny that, Ethel.

Matron Did she say that?

Ethel (*reluctantly*) Yes, I'm afraid she did. (*Violently*) Oh, damn!

Matron I must say it is a well-known fact that murderers have an urge to talk and boast of their crime. And after being reminded of it all by that programme, I suppose . . . Oh, dear, I'll have to send a report to the Board of Governors.

Ethel You can only say it is a suspicion.

Matron They will want proof. There'll be enquiries, upsets . . .

Louise Well, just ask her to leave. Say you need her room for a more deserving case. I'll get cold shivers just being in the same house as her.

Ethel Then why don't you leave?

Louise Because I've nowhere to go.

Ethel How do you know Mary has? In God's name she's paid for her crime . . .

Matron But the other residents . . . Please, please, I'll have to do something.

Louise Thank heaven for that! The sooner the better, I say.

The door opens and Mary enters complete with her knitting bag

Mary Oh, hallo, Matron!

Matron (*stuttering*) Ha—ha—hallo, Mary!

Mary moves to her chair and settles herself while the others gaze at her in a horrified silence. Mary, oblivious, placidly takes out her knitting

Mary That concert programme. So disappointing, it was

Stravinsky. Try as I might I cannot understand his music. I just had to switch it off.

There is a strained silence. Suddenly the telephone rings. They are all staring at Mary, and nobody makes a move to answer it

The telephone! Matron, don't you think you ought to . . .

Matron Oh, yes, of course. (*She goes to the telephone*) Hallo! Grantley Home. Yes . . . Who? . . . Yes, she's here. Just a moment. (*She holds out the receiver*) It's for you, Mary.

Mary Oh, thank you! (*She rises and takes the receiver from the Matron*) Hallo? . . . Oh, my dear, how lovely to hear from you. Are you well? . . . Oh, good! How are Sylvia and the children? . . . I'm so glad. Do please give them my love, bless them . . . What? . . . Well, I only saw half of it as the set broke down.

The others react

I quite agree. I felt detached from it all, too. It really was a most extraordinary feeling. I suppose it was because I couldn't associate the actors and actresses with us . . . (*She laughs*) My dear, you didn't come over at all well . . . No, dear, it didn't upset me at all. Really it didn't . . .

The others react again

Oh, Robin, I'd love to. How very sweet of you and Sylvia to ask me. You'll come and collect me? . . . Oh, thank you, my dear . . . Yes, that would make me very happy . . . Good night, my dear, and God bless you. (*She replaces the receiver and goes back to her chair*) My nephew, bless him. Matron, he'll be coming here on Friday to take me to his home for the weekend. I do so love his wife and his adorable children. Such a dear, dear boy.

Ethel Your—your—nephew?

Mary (*with a little laugh*) Yes, the one you said you wouldn't trust an inch. He's very sweet and kind, not a bit like the actor who played him.

Louise Were—were—you in the play? I mean, did somebody play you?

Mary (*surprised*) Yes, of course, but it wasn't like me either.

Matron I—I never saw it. Who were you?

Mary The murdered woman's sister. I lived with her. (*To the others*) You remember her? They called me Amy.

Ethel Yes, yes, of course, not a bit like you.

Madge Far too big and horsey looking.

They all laugh immoderately at this as the tension relaxes

Mary Seeing it brought it all back to me. I'm so sorry. I'm afraid I talked too much tonight.

Matron Nonsense! (*Archly*) I like to see my girls getting on so well together. I'm sure they enjoyed it.

Louise Oh, yes, we did. It was so interesting.

Mary That poor unfortunate woman—my sister's companion, Mary. Yes, her name was Mary, too, but as you know they called her Maud. (*She puts her hands to her mouth suddenly in horror*) Goodness gracious!

Ethel What's wrong, Mary?

Mary It's just struck me. I hope, oh, I do hope none of you thought *I* was that poor unfortunate woman. I never realized until this moment . . .

Louise Mary darling, of course not! Never for one moment. We were so interested in what you were telling us. (*Turning to the others*) Weren't we!

Madge (*laughing*) Imagine us thinking you . . .

Everybody is highly amused at the very thought

Mary Oh, I'm so glad.

Matron Now, supper! Come along all of you.

There is a general movement towards the door, led by Matron

Louise Now Matron, don't forget to ring the television people.

Matron First thing in the morning. I promise.

Ethel Coming, Mary?

Mary In a minute or two. I simply must finish this row.

All except Mary exit, and the door is closed

After a moment Mary lays her knitting down. She gazes ahead, and then slowly her hand moves and grasps the cushion beside her. She pulls it out and clutches it with both hands. A change comes over her face; it is no longer sweet

Mary (*in a tense, choked voice*) So easy to take that stupid companion's cardigan while she slept and put it on. And all for nothing! (*She suddenly raises the cushion and rams it viciously into her lap*) All for nothing! For nothing! God damn her mean soul!!

Her hands relentlessly grind into the cushion and she stares fixedly ahead, as—

the CURTAIN *slowly falls*

FURNITURE AND PROPERTY LIST

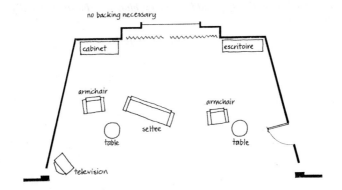

On stage: Large settee. *On it:* cushions, newspaper
2 armchairs. *On them:* cushions. *On one:* Mary's knitting
    and pattern
Escritoire. *On it:* telephone, directory. *In drawer:* pack of
    cards
2 occasional tables
Cabinet or sideboard
Television set on table
Carpet
Curtains (drawn)

Personal: **Mary:** watch
Ethel: watch

LIGHTING PLOT

Property fittings required: pendant or wall-brackets
Interior. A lounge

To open: All artificial lighting on
No cues